It was the start of another summer, and like every eight-year-old kid, I was full of excited expectations for all the great adventures ahead. I had absolute confidence these adventures were going to happen. It was starting off great with my best friend, Timmy, finally able to get a new puppy just a couple of weeks ago. Today was the first day Timmy's parents were letting him bring his new puppy to our recreation park.

My name is Rusty, and Timmy has been my best friend ever since I can remember. We both live in homes facing the Samson Recreation Park. When we were very small, both our parents would take us to the toddler's playground in the rec park, where we met and have been together almost every day since. Now that we are going into the third grade, Timmy's parents said we are finally old enough to properly take care of a dog, never doubting for a minute that I would be fully involved in this adventure.

We named him Huck after an exciting story we were told about at storybook time. He is a totally black Labrador and right now just all paws and head. Today we were going to teach Huck the basics, how to stay and come on command.

It was Sunday, and I was swinging on the monkey gym like every Sunday, waiting for Timmy and family to get home from church. I am pretty good on the bars, and my mom says I am like a monkey. Besides, it's the best viewing point to watch for Timmy's big blue family car drive into their driveway. They just got home fifteen minutes ago, so I knew Timmy would be coming down the driveway any minute, probably with Sherry and Betsy, his two older sisters, also coming to the rec park.

After Timmy and Huck checked in with Debbie, our park monitor for today, they came charging toward me at a full run. I jumped to the ground, grabbed my backpack, and started to run. We veered off in unison and headed for the top of the hill, which is our normal turf for eating lunch. The race to the top was always our contest, but once made, we never dwelled on it. We plopped down under our tree and let Huck jump wildly all over us as we laughed. We already knew our plan of attack for the day—to introduce Huck to all aspects of the rec park, so we got busy pulling our lunch out of our packs and laying out treasured goodies to share. We had just started munching down when I remembered with excitement where my mom had offered to take us.

"Timmy, guess what! My mom said she will take us to the lake the last Sunday this month to go fishing! She said we will leave in the morning around eight thirty. Do you think you can come? We will be back by suppertime."

"That sounds great! But I can't go on Sunday because we have church."

"Can you miss church this one time?"

Without hesitation of any kind, Timmy replied, "No. I'm sure I can't. My parents always tell us out of all the things we are learning, that learning about God is the most important. That is why we never miss a Sunday to learn about him."

I was arrested to silence. I had never heard Timmy talk this way, with a steely confidence that nothing would change mainly because it was what he was feeling and not just his parents. We had never talked about God or what he learned at church.

Quickly to assure him, I said, "I will ask Mom if she could take us on the last Saturday."

Timmy turned from placing Huck into a sitting position and with a huge smile on his face, said, "Oh, that would be so grand! We could even row a boat out to fish in the deeper part."

I started laughing. "Now that you think you are an expert rower after our last practice trip to the pond!" and it was done. All I had to do was convince Mom to go on Saturday.

We spent the rest of the day with Huck chasing us around the rec park and failing miserably to teach him to stay on command. But it was a rollicking day that we all enjoyed, and it ended when Debbie sounded the supper horn. I said goodbye to Timmy and Huck at the monitoring table and plopped down on the grass, watching the clouds, waiting for Mom to come and fetch me.

I was thinking back to what Timmy said about God. In truth, I never really stopped thinking about it all day. Of course, I had heard the word *God* many times, and I knew what church was, but I really knew nothing about either one. I had never been to church, and Mom never talked about God. I wondered, were we missing something very important? What exactly was God? As hard as I tried, I could not even begin to imagine.

Later at supper, after I had told Mom all about the funny things Huck had done. I looked at Mom and asked, "Mom, what is God?"

She looked up with surprise, then I could tell she was thinking very hard. Slowly and thoughtfully, she said,

WHAT IS GOD?

A Rusty's Neighborhood Series

Joyce Bolton

GOLD SEAL OF EXCELLENCE

★ ARPRESS ★

TOP-RATED BOOK

ARPress

ARPress
45 Dan Road Suite 5
Canton MA 02021
Hotline: 1(888) 821-0229
Fax: 1(508) 545-7580

Ordering Information:
Quantity sales. Special discounts are available on quantity purchases by corporations, associations, and others. For details, contact the publisher at the address above.

Printed in the United States of America.

ISBN-13:   Softcover   979-8-89676-419-9
                eBook   979-8-89676-420-5

Library of Congress Control Number: 20259108547

"Hmm, that is quite a question." After more pause, she said, "I don't think I have a good answer."

We both sat there looking at each other in thought. She then said, "What made you ask about God?"

"Well, today Timmy said his parents told him that learning about God is the most important learning we could do. Oh, that reminds me, can we go to the lake on Saturday instead of Sunday because Timmy must go to church on Sundays?"

With a big smile on her face that pleased me very much, she said, "Oh I see. Well, we will just have to see if Frank can take us in his RV on Saturday. Not to worry, I will convince him."

We ate the rest of our supper in silence and then suddenly Mom jumped up and said, "I've got an idea!" then promptly ran to her office space and brought back her big whiteboard and propped it up on its easel next to the table. I watched in fascination as she wrote at the top, "What is God?"

She turned to me with excitement and asked, "Rusty, why don't you and I make a project out of it?"

"A project? What do you mean a project?"

"Well, it seems that neither one of us really knows exactly what God is, so as beginners, we might start our project of finding out by asking others what they think

God is. Each of us can go out each day and during the day, ask people we know what they think God is. Then we can write their answers on the board each night and discuss what they mean. After we have gathered enough information, maybe we will learn a clue on what we should do next. What do you think? Are you up for the challenge?"

Everything inside me came alive. It was like we were going on a treasure hunt together! I jumped up and ran to hug my mother. I felt like a big person, and together we are going to really find the answer.

"Mom, this is the best idea ever!" and together we laughed and stated to dance around in a circle.

Monday morning, Mom called from the kitchen, "Rusty, are you ready?"

"Coming," as I ran down the hallway. Mom was just closing my pack. "I made your favorite chicken sandwich today, and I put a whole bag of puppy treats for Huck." She held the bag open. "Here, put your glove in." Today was our Little League practice.

We were both out the door speed walking to Patsy's house a block away. When we arrived at Patsy's door, my mom gave me my morning hug goodbye and whispered in my ear, "Remember our project."

"Yes, I will."

She gave me a wink and ran off to catch her ride to work.

Every morning, I helped Patsy cart her yoga class equipment to the rec park, pulling one of her two wagons. She started her class at nine every morning, so I helped her set up her class and stayed with her until the park monitors arrived on duty at ten o'clock. Since I must stay with her, I just figure I would do the yoga with her class every day, which made me pretty good at it by now.

Last night, I thought about who I knew that I might ask about God, and of course, Patsy was at the top of the list. Patsy was one of the kindest grown-ups I knew, so I knew I wanted to ask her what she thought.

"Patsy, can I ask you a question?"

"Of course you can. What is it?"

"Can you tell me what God is?"

She stopped and looked at me with a hint of a smile on her face and said, "My, what a big question."

She sat down on her mat and pointed to mine to follow. Thoughtfully she repeated my question, "So you want to know what God is." Pausing and looking right at me, she said with a big smile, "God is the source of life."

This took me by total surprise, but after a few moments, I blurted out, "Does that mean he makes everything that is alive? How does he do this?"

Patsy smiled and said, "God is not a man. God is the source of all life like the sun is the source of all light."

I sat there trying to picture the sun and its giving off light, but I did not really understand God giving life, and Patsy could see my puzzlement on my face. She said, "That is why Jesus told us we need to build on our relationship with God every day, and through that relationship, God will teach us more and more of the answers. It's a process. We must learn to love God, and in doing that, we learn about God's love for us and his power."

"How do we do that?"

"This is how, searching for the truth. You are just starting with your project. Keep asking the questions in your project with your mother. You will find the next step."

I asked, "I can have a relationship with God?"

"You already do, but you are just now starting to participate in it. Keep it up." After a few moments of thought, she got up and said, "You think on what we talked about for a while and keep me posted as you learn more."

It was time for her class to start, and as I went through the motions, I came to the conclusion that there probably are many pieces to this puzzle, and I would have to gather more information before things started to make sense to me, so I decided that even if I didn't completely understand the answers, I would just remember them so I could share them with Mom at the end of the day. Maybe we needed to see many answers before we would figure this out.

When Timmy arrived at the rec park at his usual time, ten, he had Huck with him. It took us two minutes to decide that with the growing heat of the day, we should head for the pond shallows. The shallows was the entire west end of the pond that extended out in very shallow waters, just perfect for running around in and splashing everyone, and we loved to play team keep-away with a Nerf ball. When we arrived, we found Sam, Ralph, and Buzz, who were already engaged in a game of pushover. They were all three on the same Little League baseball team as Timmy and I, so we charged into the water to join in the fun. I think Huck was having the most fun, but by lunch, we were all totally soaked, muddy, and completely happy. We tried to lay out on the grass to get sun dried before time to run over to the baseball diamonds for practice.

After baseball practice, I told Timmy I would meet him and Huck at the refreshments stand and ran over to talk to Riley, who was one of our coaches.

"Riley, can I ask you a very important question?"

He looked at me with a chuckle. "Oh, an important question?"

Riley was kind of a teaser, so I tried to use my serious voice. "Yes, I think it is a very important question."

Riley closed the bat bag and led me over to the bench. "Okay, Rusty, if it is important, let's sit down and you can tell me about it."

I sat down on the bench and just blurted out my question, "What is God?"

I knew that was surprise on his face, but then it changed to that kind face I knew so well. "Rusty, that is indeed an important question and one I think about all the time. I am honored you asked my opinion. I'll tell you what I know for sure—that God is all-powerful."

"All powerful?"

"Yes, he is the only true power in everyone's life and the world. But this is something you can remember now and always: the more you know about God, the stronger you will feel and the less fear you will feel. So keep on this quest."

"Does God give you strength?"

"Yes, he gives us inner strength in every situation." He then took my baseball cap out of my hands and put it on my head, tapping the bill. As he stood up, he said, "You think on that a while for I know it to be true."

I jumped up. "Thanks, Riley. I'll see you on Wednesday," and ran off to join up with Timmy.

Timmy, Huck, and I spent the rest of the day getting completely filthy playing at the pond till Timmy had to go home. I finally had a chance to think over what I learned today while I lay on the grass at the monitor station waiting for Mom to pick me up. I couldn't wait to tell her what I learned, and we both laughed very hard when that was exactly what we both said to each other when she arrived.

Mom said, "Okay, let's do this right and wait to tell each other what we learned until we can write it on our project board."

Later, after we ate, Mom pulled the board over to the table. "You go first."

"Patsy says God is the creator of all life. She says he is the source like the sun is to light. Riley says God is all powerful and learning about God will give us strength inside. He also said learning more about God will remove fear."

Mom wrote them on the board, then she said, "Amy said God is good. Actually, she said God is only good, all goodness."

We studied what we put on the board for a few minutes and then Mom asked me what I thought about them.

"Maybe if we put them together like a sentence…"

"Rusty, you are brilliant!" and she promptly got up and went to her desk and came back with Post-its. "Let's write them on Post-its and then we can move them around to make new sentences. We can write the sentences in line below."

11

After working at different combinations, we came up with these: God is an all-powerful god that is the source of all life. The only power is God, and it is always good. God is the creator of everything, and it is always good. God removes fear.

I looked at Mom and said, "God sounds pretty important. Do you think it is true?"

She looked back at me and said, "I don't know. I think that is what we must figure out. Let's get more input tomorrow, okay?"

"Okay. It was kind of fun, like I was on a mission."

The next day while helping Patsy set up, I asked her, "Patsy how do you know this about God is true?"

Patsy replied, "Because as you grow in your knowledge and relationship with God, you begin to prove its truth."

"Really?"

"Absolutely. It is so powerful it changes you and the world around you. Best of all, you become happy."

"But, Patsy, I already am happy."

"That is wonderful, but this is a special happiness that grows inside you so that you are the source of happiness, and you bring joy to others just being around you."

Now this was interesting to me. Patsy's yoga class was starting, so I went to my matt, but I thought on this happy person idea. Timmy was a very happy person, and I wondered maybe that was from his learning of God. I could think of hundreds of times in our years of friendship when it was his happiness that I wanted to be near.

I met Timmy after yoga class, and after playing chase with Huck, we headed off to the park center to the craft workshop. Tuesday was our day in crafts workshop, and we were learning how to mix finger paints to make different colors. Huck ended up with a few different color spots on his black fur before we were finished, but he wore them proudly. I couldn't stop laughing when I looked over at Timmy and his nose was blue. At the end of our session, Timmy said he was going to the hose to give Huck and himself a wash down, so I decided to go talk to our teacher, Sarah.

Sarah chuckled when I came near and said, "Hi, Rusty, you and Timmy really looked like you were having fun today!"

I felt a bit guilty because Timmy and I really had been extra crazy today. Sara just laughed and said, "That is okay. Painting is supposed to be fun, so it makes me happy to see when you are enjoying yourselves."

"Sarah, I was wondering if you could help me with a project I am doing with my mom?"

"Oh that sounds fun. What is it?"

"We are asking people we know what they think God is."

"Oh, my favorite subject!" Then she sat on her stool and thought, repeating to herself, "What do I think God is…" After a short pause, her face lit up, and she said, "God is all-knowing. God knows everything."

"Really? So he knows more than everyone?"

"Yes, and that is why you can always trust in God."

"What do you mean trust in him?"

"Well, if you keep learning and learn to speak with God each day, you can trust he will always help you find the answers."

As I thought over what she just said, I realized I did not know how to speak with God.

Sara responded, "Do you remember I am always telling all my students that continual practice makes you better at painting, drawing, building, and every skill we try new in workshop?"

After I nodded yes, Sara went on, "Well, it's the same with God. You must practice learning, talking, and listening to God every day, and that makes you better and better at it."

"Do you mean I can practice talking to God right away and I will get better at it?"

"Absolutely, always speak from your heart. But remember the key to talking with God is learning how to listen and hear God. You start improving when you learn the principles of God." Sara could see I was confused about the principles, and she added, "This is what you have been doing with your project. You have just begun to gather the principles of God. It's a great project, and I hope you keep it up."

Timmy popped around the corner. "Hey, Rusty, come on. We are all clean, and we need to hurry to soccer."

Sarah said, "Rusty, you and your mom think on what we talked about and let me know how your project goes. Bye now."

"Thanks, Sarah!" and off I ran with Timmy and Huck, racing to the soccer fields.

Soccer practice was a lot of fun today because our coach was rotating me into all the forward positions and using two balls today, which meant I was seeing a lot of action.

After practice, Alice, our assistant coach, stayed to eat lunch on the grass while waiting for the next team to start practice. Timmy, Huck, and I decided to eat with her because she had a large jug of Kool-Aid and yummy brownies. Timmy decided to try to dribble a ball through the obstacle course with Huck, so that left me alone with Alice. You guessed it, I decided to ask Alice my project question.

Without even hesitating, Alice said, "God is love and the source of all love."

Here was that source thing again—first, the source of life, then goodness, and now love. I realized I did not know what love was.

"My mom tells me she loves me, and I hear people say 'I love you' on TV and around, but when I think about it, I don't really know what it is. I think it is liking something a lot."

Alice smiled and said, "Well, that is true, but there are many kinds of love. To begin to grow in love, you must exercise love, and the more you exercise it, the better you get at it. But everyone is born with the capacity to love because it is given by God. And love is magic. It heals every situation and heals the world. Everyone wants to be loved, feel loved, and a chance to give love."

"So you are saying I already know how to love even though I am not sure what love is."

"Yes, and that is because we all get it through God."

"How do you know love is from God?"

"It is from God because it is limitless, meaning you can always love more."

I sat there in silence thinking about what she said. Both of us watched Timmy and Huck fall over each other and the ball, laughing the entire time when Alice said softly but confidently, "Rusty, you know how to love. You love your friends Timmy and Huck."

I looked at her, and she winked at me with a smile. "And they love you."

She got up to start picking up and said, "You can thank God for that truly wonderful miracle, but most important of all, God always loves you, and that never changes." Handing me the last of the brownies, she said, "Here, take the last two brownies for you and Timmy." Then she added, "You know that project you are doing with your mom is pretty cool, and she is showing you how much she loves you by doing it."

I hadn't thought about that before, but when Alice said it, it made me feel really good inside. We said goodbye to Alice and thanked her for the munchies and headed over to the pond. All our friends were there, and we spent the rest of the day laughing while getting completely wet and muddy from head to toe.

When Mom met me at the park to walk me home, she laughed when she saw me and said, "Looks like you had a very fun day!" As we walked home, Mom was looking down at me with a smirk on her face. "Well, Mr. Mudpie, I think a good long bath is first order of business for you."

Looking up at her, I said, "I learned a lot about what God is today."

"Me too. How about let's talk about our findings over some cabbage burgers?"

"Yeah! You know I love cabbage burgers!"

Mom answered with, "I'll race you home!" and started to take off running. I charged after her, determined to beat her this time.

Cabbage burgers was one of both our favorites, so we were halfway through with our burgers before we started our project daily findings. Mom moved the white board next to the table and said, "Okay, you go first. What did you learn today?"

"Sarah said God is all-knowing. She says God knows everything all the time. What was real neat was that she said God will talk to me, that I could learn to have a relationship with God, and he will teach me."

My mom looked fascinated and asked, "Well, how are you supposed to start this relationship?"

"Sarah says I already have a relationship with God, but we don't know it because we don't know about God. She says our project is the way to start, and we must keep learning about God's principles, and we will learn how to be a part of this relationship."

"So she thinks we are doing the right thing and that by learning more about God, we will become closer to God?"

I nodded my head yes, taking another bite from my burger.

"Well, that is interesting and surprisingly logical." She wrote on the board *all-knowing*, and then next to it *teacher and friend*.

"Anything else?"

"Yes. Alice says God is love. She says God is the source of all love, and there is no stopping limit to love."

Mom, listening intently, responded, "Yes, that is very powerful, isn't it? Diane told me the same thing today. Diane says that is why all of us, even animals, naturally have the capacity to love."

"Is love when you like someone a lot?"

Mom was pondering this and then she set her burger down and leaned forward to look me in the face. "I used to think I knew what love was, but when I had you, I realized I had never loved anything before you with that much intensity and absolutely no effort to do so. When I held you for the first time, the love overwhelmed me and brought tears to my eyes. We had just met, and my love was immediate. I knew it would be forever no matter what. Now that I have watched you grow into who you are today, my love for you keeps growing. So I understand when Alice says no limit to love. Diane says God is true love and his love is so much more powerful and intense that we cannot ever imagine it."

I was so fascinated with my mom's story that I forgot about my burger and was drawn to my mother with every muscle of my being, and I realized at that moment that I loved my mother very much. We were staring at each other for a while, then broke into a big smile and said as she began to write on the board, "God is love."

I was studying the board and said, "I think, so far, those are my favorite two."

Mom responded, "I like them also. Both are very comforting."

Finishing up on my burger I asked, "So what did you learn?"

"Well, I told you about Diane, but I also talked to Brad on the bus ride home. He said that God was eternal."

"What does that mean?"

"It means God is forever and consistent."

As she was writing this on the board, I was thinking, "So does that mean love is forever also?"

My mom turned to me with a surprised expression. "Well, I guess it does!" Then after thinking on what we learned, she said, "How about let's gather more information for one more day and then we can really talk about what we want to do? Don't you have your practice races tomorrow?"

"Yes, Mr. Johnson will be at the park tomorrow, and we are practicing our relay races for our big track meet."

"Do you know who is on your relay teams and which races you are in?"

"No, he will help us form our teams tomorrow. I was thinking he will be good to ask about God because I know he prays to God all the time, and maybe he can tell me about praying also."

Mom looked pleased. "Oh, that sounds good. I don't know much about praying, so that will help us." We shook hands on the plan as we both grabbed fudge bars out of the freezer.

The next day, Timmy arrived earlier as planned because Mr. Johnson always started on time in school, and we didn't want to miss out on getting on a good fast team. Mr. Johnson, who was our elementary physical education teacher, always puts on a big summertime track meet, and it was a very big deal to win one of the events. This year he announced that all the relay races were going to be both boys and girls on each team. Timmy and I knew right away that we wanted Peggy and Dorie, who were twins that just moved here last year. They were both very fast. We were thinking they would be our secret weapons. They were supposed to meet us at the racing area.

I was pretty excited because there were so many teams formed up to compete. We were team 12, and Ralph and Buzz were on team 14. They also had Carol, who was a very fast girl, and I knew they would be hard to beat. This was our first day of practice, so each team had a chance to decide which three races they wanted to compete in after practicing out of six events.

Ralph and Buzz's team were only competing in two events like many, but Peggy and Dorie were real competitors and convinced Timmy and I that we could do good in three events. All of us decided we were going to practice our racing Thursday morning so we could be ready for Friday's first trial. On Friday, Mr. Johnson would run us through a full meet with all the races and all the teams. The big race event was two Fridays away.

We were all eating our lunch on the hill when I finally saw my chance to talk to Mr. Johnson. He was setting out his lunch on the registration table. I told my friends I would be back, I wanted to talk to Mr. Johnson about something, and ran down the hill.

"Hi, Mr. Johnson. I was hoping to talk with you about something kind of important."

"Hi, Rusty, sure. What is this important topic?"

"My mom and I are doing a project together on God."

Mr. Johnson leaned back in surprise and smiled, saying, "Well, that truly is important! How can I help?"

"Our project is trying to learn what God is, so we each are asking people we know what they think God is. What do you think God is?"

"Well, I will tell you something about God that many people do not consider or understand, but it is very important."

"What is that?"

He said very slowly so that I would remember, "God is spiritual."

I just looked at him with a blank face. I had no idea what he meant or was talking about.

Mr. Johnson smiled and said, "Here, sit down for a minute and let's talk." I did so when next he said, "*Spirit* means 'without any material limitations or boundaries.'"

I could not imagine what he was describing and said, "I don't understand."

"Okay, think of the number 5. Do you see it in your thoughts?"

"Yes, I see a number 5."

"Now change it to number 4."

"I see a number 4."

"Change it back to number 5. How fast were you able to make that change?"

"Instantly."

"That's right, and how many times do you think you can think of number 5 before you use them all up?"

I chuckled. "Never. I can think of number 5 every day forever."

"That is right, and is the number 5 perfect every time you think of it?"

I snickered. "Yes."

"Yes, it is never tired or sick?"

I was laughing now. "No, it is never sick or tired."

"Now make your five red."

"It's red."

"Turn it green."

Laughing, I said it was green now.

"What we have been doing is living in the spiritual. There are no limitations or boundaries of any kind."

I sat there thinking a while when Mr. Johnson said, "God is Spirit. This is a new concept for you and will need a lot more thinking on it. But remember"—he paused for emphasis—"this is one of the most important keys to understanding God. Think about all the limitless power your thoughts have. That is only a speck of what God's full being is."

I felt I was on the edge of some magical discovery that excited me, but I was not quite sure what. "How will I lean more about this?"

"Learning about God is a journey that each one of us needs to travel to get closer to God and the truth. You are just starting, so taking baby steps is what almost all of us must do. The secret is to keep learning each week. I will give you two more things to think about. Music is spiritual, and love is spiritual. I'll make a deal with you. After the track meet is over, we can meet again here in the park, and you can tell me what you have learned about God and Spirit. Is that a deal?"

"Yes!" and we shook hands on it.

"Thanks, Mr. Johnson. You have given me a lot to think about, and I hope I can explain it to my mom!"

He laughed. "I look forward to our next talk." I got up to run back to my friends, waving goodbye to Mr. Johnson.

After lunch, we all decided to have an all-out race to the baseball field. All eight of us lined up to start. Buzz yelled "Go!" and we were off! I was laughing so hard, my eyes started to water, but Timmy and I were neck and neck, and we had no idea where everyone else was till we broke through to the open field area leading to the diamonds. To my surprise, all three girls were just ahead of us now. The first one to touch the fence backdrop was the winner.

We all crashed into it and fell to the ground laughing. We finally agreed Dorie was the winner, and I decided we actually might win on race day.

During practice, something interesting happened that made me think about what Mr. Johnson had told me. Brent was always having problems hitting the ball, and today he was about to give up. But Mr. Riley came over and got down on one knee to look at Brent in the face. He said, "Brent, I want you to close your eyes and picture yourself standing at the plate ready for a pitch." Brent closed his eyes.

"Do you see yourself?"

"Yes."

"Now you are watching for the pitch. The ball is released and coming to you. You are watching the ball come, and now you swing the bat still watching the ball. The bat comes around, and you see the bat hit the ball. You feel and hear it connect. Then finish the swing." Mr. Riley waited a minute. "Did you see yourself hit the perfect hit?"

Brent answered, "Yes."

"Do it again. Start from the stance and watch the ball all the way to a perfect hit." We all watched Brent with his eyes closed, seeing himself swing and hit the ball in his thoughts. Brent then responded, "Yes. I hit the ball hard."

Mr. Riley said, "Good. Now there is no reason in the world you cannot do exactly the same hit when you step up to the plate. I want you to see it in your mind one more time and then step up to the plate and do it for real."

We all watched him with his eyes closed then step up to the plate. The pitch came, and Brent swung and hit the ball square on into the right field. It was the best hit I had ever seen Brent make, and he was ecstatic. We all were. As I sat on the bench waiting for my turn, I thought back to what Mr. Johnson had said, that being in our thoughts is like being in the spiritual, with no limitations, and that is what God is all the time. But Mr. Riley helped Brent use his spiritual picture to take away his limitations for real. This was all new to me, and I hoped that Mom could help figure this out. I just hoped I could explain it all to her.

Later while I was lying on the grass staring up at the clouds, my mom's face appeared above me and she said, "Boo!"

I started laughing and said, "You didn't scare me!"

Laughing hard, she challenged me, "Ready to race me home? Ready, set, *go!*" and she was off. I did my best to beat her. She slowed down to let me get even with her and then zoomed ahead when we got closer to home.

"We are having spaghetti and meatballs tonight, and I hope you have something special you learned about God to tell me."

"Yeah! Spaghetti! And Mr. Johnson had a doozy."

Mom said, "Oh, goodie. Quick with your bath. I'll make dinner." When sitting down to eat, Mom pulled the whiteboard over to the table so we could read over what we had so far learned.

"So what did Mr. Johnson have to say?"

"He told me God is spiritual, without limitations or boundaries, and perfect."

My mom pondered, "Without limitations or boundaries and perfect. That is interesting. I always think of *spiritual* as meaning no material form. I guess that is true that the material form is what creates all the limits and boundaries."

"Mr. Johnson said this was an important key concept about God." I talked my mom through the same number 5 steps that Mr. Johnson took me through and told her this was an example of the spiritual. My mom sat there quietly thinking for some time and then she looked up at me and excitedly said, "You know, I think Mr. Johnson might be trying to tell us not to make the mistake of trying to understand God based upon the life dimensions we understand. And that we will never understand God unless we understand the principles of this spiritual being. The closest we can understand this spiritual realm is the example of where our thoughts exist and the unlimited freedom we have there."

"What do you mean 'life dimensions we understand'?"

"We all live under the physical laws of a material universe, like time, gravity, conflict, pain, death, limited supply, decay, etc., and those are the things we understand."

After a few moments of thought, I responded, "So Mr. Johnson is saying God doesn't have any of those things, and that is why we have a hard time understanding God."

My mom said, "Yes. I think that is why Mr. Johnson is saying this is a key to understanding God."

I added, "Mr. Johnson says we each have our own journey to follow in our search for God. Everyone keeps telling me to get there we must keep working on it every week."

Mom said, "Yes, it appears we must do the work. Maybe that is why Timmy's parents set so much importance on not missing Sunday church—to ensure he sets aside the time to keep learning about God."

We sat thinking a few minutes in silence and then we both spoke at the same time, "So do you want to keep learning about God?" We both laughed, and Mom said, "Tell me what you want to do."

I knew immediately what I wanted to do, but I looked into the face of my mom hoping she would feel the same. I knew I could not do it without her, and I felt so much closer to her these past few days than ever before, so I took a deep breath and said, "I have liked learning about God so far, and I want to learn more. I would always feel we missed something very important if we did not keep going."

I did not realize how much this was beginning to mean to me until my mom answered, "Okay that settles it. We keep learning." We both got up and gave each other a big bear hug.

We separated, and I looked into her face. "What do we do next?"

"Do you remember my friend Cynthia who has the home on the lake? We spent the weekend riding in her boats the entire time?"

"How could I forget. That was so much fun!"

"Well, I have been talking to her about our project, and she was very supportive of it. She asked me if I knew what we planned to do next if we decided to keep learning more about God. I told her, not a clue. She then asked us both to come to her house for the whole weekend and she would teach us how to sail. She also said maybe we could talk about what to do next while we were enjoying ourselves on the lake. Would you like that?"

"Yes, would I ever!"

"Good, she said she would have all their water toys ready for us!"

"Oh boy, that is going to be really fun. I love their sailboat!"

The next two days seemed to fly by, maybe because they were so action packed with fun or maybe because I had started to study Timmy a lot more closely because I knew he was ahead of me in knowing about God. I had always just accepted and enjoyed our friendship, but now I was realizing how special it was, and that was largely because of Timmy. I was noticing that it was not just me that was attracted to Timmy's effervescent joy in everything we did and also his ability to make everyone feel special in their own individual way. I wondered if this was what happened when you got closer to God. Patsy had said that getting closer to God made you happier inside, and I knew from watching Timmy if that was true, then that was something I wanted to feel myself always.

I was so excited for our trip to the lake on Saturday that I was up earlier than usual, but I guess Mom was also because she was already up and in the kitchen. When she saw me, she laughed and said, "Were you too excited to sleep?"

"Yes! I can't wait to get there. How long do you think it will take?"

"Well, since I rented us a car last night, maybe only a thirty-five-minute drive." Laughing she added, "I already put our bags in the car."

After a good breakfast, we were on the road. Cynthia lived on a big recreation lake that was shaped like a boomerang, which gave a lot of lake to explore, especially in a sailboat. Cynthia and family had their own dock with several different types of water toys, but when she asked me which one I wanted to go on first that Saturday morning, I promptly said the sailboat. I loved any boat on the water, but for some reason, the fact that you used sails to angle against the wind allowing you to navigate a course and the knowledge of how to do that fascinated me—that and the feeling of being so close to the water that you could touch the water with your hand over the side.

Cynthia knew I ached to learn the secrets to sailing, so she let me take charge of the tiller while she worked the sails. As we moved through the water, she taught me how the sails used the wind and its relationship with the tiller.

We sailed all morning, ate lunch on her deck, and then back out on the lake in the afternoon to test what I learned. We were on a long tack headed back home when Cynthia asked, "So how is your project coming?"

My mom and I looked at each other and then Mom said, "Rusty, why don't you share what you think with Cynthia?"

Well, I felt pretty special in this grown-up conversation and the fact they wanted to hear my opinions on this important subject, so I really searched my true feelings inside.

"We started the project to find out what God was."

Cynthia said, "And did you find out?"

"We found out what others think God is, but they were each telling us only one part of God, a part that they found important themselves."

Cynthia asked, "What did you think about their answers? Did you learn something?"

"God is not simple to understand. Each answer was something so much bigger than I had expected."

Cynthia, "By 'big,' do you mean powerful? Like something that can affect your life?"

"Yes, very big things that affect your life but in really good ways. Like God loves us and wants to help us, but we must make him our friend."

Cynthia, smiling with her whole face, said, "Yes, I think we need to make God our friend."

I then asked her, "Are you friends with God?"

Cynthia answered, "Yes, I love God."

Mom then asked, "How do you love God?"

Cynthia said, "That is a great question. Jesus told us how to love God. One way is to love one another. That is why I want to help you."

Mom asked, "But how do you know God is real? What is the benefit of loving God?"

Cynthia answered, "I know God is real because I have seen and experienced the changes it has made in my life and with my family. The more you learn about God and his goodness, the more you begin to feel his presence and start to recognize his power in your life. You see through a changed heart. It gives you faith, and the doubts leave you." She went on to say, "When Jesus came to teach the Hebrews about God, they all expected God to fix their present existence. But Jesus tried to teach them that God has always been there and will always be there, but each one of us must make the journey to find God. You must become the light of your own life. And you start this with love."

Cynthia walked us through a tack as we were getting close to the shoreline, and when she settled on the other side of the boat, she looked at both of us and said, "Let me ask you this. You know the power of love. You have seen the power of love and felt it." She paused as Mom nodded yes in response and then said, "God is love. Now is love real?"

I looked at my mom and found her looking at me. After a few minutes, I said to her, "Mom, from doing this project in finding God with you, I have learned that I love you."

My mom reached over and pulled me into a big hug and then, laughing, said, "Okay, what do we do next?"

The End

About the Author

Joyce Bolton lives in Florida, where she enjoys running, biking, golfing, and all water sports in the beautiful warm waters of the Gulf of Mexico, not to mention the pleasures of wearing shorts every day of the year. Joyce graduated with a bachelor of science degree from the Colorado State University and spent the first eleven years teaching and coaching before transitioning to the business world for the last thirty years; however, she says teaching was her true calling. Her daily motto is to listen to great music, fill your day with laughter, and always do the right thing.